Introduction

Just over 30 years ago, the first edition of 60 Plans for Small Railways appeared and proved an instant success. It was a compilation of plans I had drawn for RAILWAY MODELLER that fell into a rather loosely defined space limit, basically up to 8ft × 6ft maximum, or L shaped portable layouts and terminus plans. Three editions then followed, by which time the origination was getting more than a little tired and so it was decided that the plans needed redrawing. At the same time, it seemed advisable to bring them up to date.

The majority of the plans were drawn before 1960 whilst steam traction was still the norm and the branch lines and secondary routes swept away in the wake of the Beeching reorganisation were still there to inspire the modeller. This naturally biased the schemes to steam age designs. In the 1950s and '60s the majority of modellers had not merely a restricted choice of models, but also had a much lower number of locomotives in their personal collection. A responsible designer took this into account. Today, the situation is different, and so, when redrawing the plans, the only real restriction I have had to bear in mind is one of space.

This is one area where the situation has not improved. Present day houses are not as spacious as their 1930s predecessors, and worse still modern lofts are far from ideal as sites for layouts. However, there has been one area where we have added scope, the garage.

I could turn half my garage over to a layout, and still park the car inside, with its bonnet tucked neatly under a baseboard set at a comfortable height above the floor. I mention this to explain why so many plans in this book are for an 8ft wide space: they are designed to go along the back of the garage and leave room for a small to medium sized car.

As in the original books, a number of plans are shown on sectional baseboards. In many cases, the basic unit is only 3ft long, for it is, in my opinion, unwise for the individual modeller, working on his or her own, to use a module that cannot be easily carried through a normal home by one person, and, into the bargain, stored away in a reasonable area. Baseboards of this size are also much easier to fit into the back of the family car.

Most plans have one side of the drawing labelled 'FRONT', this being the side I fe... ho... po... the... sid..., ... cases, this makes the fiddle yard more accessible to the operator. I have expanded on this point in the accompanying text.

I have included three plans specifically drawn for Continental layouts. Two are based on Swiss practice, a reflection of my growing interest in the railways of that country, the other is more general in its application. I have also expanded the section on fiddle yards, a very important aspect of post-war British model railway practice.

All layouts are designed for 4mm scale, OO gauge, and the pointwork is set out to use Peco Setrack and Streamline products, not through any ruling of the publisher, but because this is the largest and most readily obtainable range of ready made track in Britain and therefore the most probable choice of the reader. I have throughout quoted the minimum radius of the design since this can affect the choice of rolling stock. As I feel the majority of readers will lean heavily towards modern ready-to-run stock, I have chosen a 1ft 3in absolute minimum, and have regarded 2ft as the optimum choice where space is available. It is advisable to set out the layout full size before construction begins. The PECO Turnout & Crossing Plan templates will greatly assist here and these are available from the manufacturers direct. It is a good idea to paste them on stiff card before cutting out to make manipulation much easier.

It goes without saying that every layout in this book could be greatly improved if only the space available were larger. Any increase in train length is highly desirable, and easing of the tighter curves will also help. However, the small schemes have their advantages; only the solid 8ft × 4ft schemes have any trackage outside comfortable reach and if, in their suggested garage location, provision is made for moving the entire layout forward, to give maintenance space at the back, even this problem is readily overcome.

Many schemes are almost all railway and in those where scenic features are incuded, I have in the main been concerned either to frame the railway itself or to provide lineside features which give rise to traffic.

C. J. Freezer
Hemel Hempstead

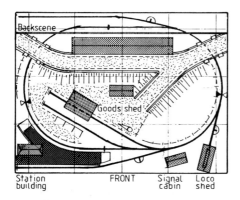

Plan No. SP1:

4ft 6in × 3ft 3in:

Minimum radius 1ft 3in

Station building   FRONT   Signal cabin   Loco shed

1: Simple Beginnings

The traditional starting point in the hobby is the train set: it was so in my youth, and it is even more true today when even the 'toylike' *Thomas the Tank Engine* sets are made up from models which are far more prototypical than most of the offerings of the 30s. The standard set contains an oval of track and possibly some points. This track is generally laid on the floor, but before long the idea of fixing it to a permanent baseboard arises. Plan SP1 shows an elementary system which, whilst only a couple of steps removed from the toy, is capable of getting near to prototypical operation and only needs a 4ft 6in by 3ft 3in baseboard. The only catch is that it is a biased system, and works best when the trains run anti-clockwise around the circuit.

The illusion of reality is enhanced by the provision of a backscene behind which we have a lie-by siding. This permits the user to have two trains on the layout, though clearly only one can run at a time. The goods facilities are enough to allow some interesting shunting, whilst there is a small loco shed which will just hold a tank loco. Indeed, it would make a good home for Thomas! Although I have not shown any track sections, it is a layout that can readily be made from standard sectional track. Indeed, I would advise the use of standard sectional curves on this, and all other layouts using 1ft 3in and 1ft 6in nominal radii, for no matter how carefully one lays flexible track, one cannot approach the accuracy of the commercial curves, made in costly, high precision tools. At such sharp radii, there is no margin for error.

SP2 is more spectacular, but gives rather less operational potential. The continuous run is looped over itself in the looped eight formation. Unfortunately, there is only scope for a single train on this line and I have suggested a mineral-only line. The sketch shows a conventional goods shed at the lower level and a set of coal drops at the upper level.

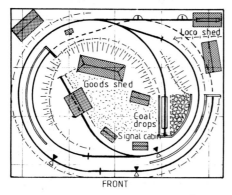

Plan No. SP2:
4ft 6in × 3ft 3in:
Minimum radius 1ft 3in

FRONT

2

Plan No. SP3:

6ft 0in × 3ft 3in:

Minimum radius 1ft 3in

Signal cabin

Factory

Farm

Station building

Signal cabin

Water tank

Cattle   FRONT   Coal Loco shed

With a little more room it is possible to produce a rather better layout and in SP3 we have a very small out-and-back layout. It is shown in two parts because the terminus is, in practice, a separate unit built on a removable board 6ft long and 1ft 3in wide, to allow access to the lower tracks for maintenance.

The high level terminus is reasonably conventional: the facilities are limited and trains cannot exceed two coaches in length. The low level loop is a little tight as drawn; it might be possible to extend this by using a curved point at the left hand end.

Although this layout can be made to dismantle, it is essentially one which will normally stand erected on trestles, ready for instant use. This is not normally possible: the majority of layouts need to be put away after running, and whilst some

writers glibly talk of putting it under the bed, they seem totally unaware not only that most modern beds have little ground clearance and six legs, but in the few cases where it is possible, the major objection is that a lot of fluff is deposited under beds, and does absolutely no good to a model railway.

A better solution is to construct the layout on several small boards which can be more readily stowed away. SP4 is just such a layout, built on two pairs of rectangular boards. Since the boards are paired, they can be stored face-to-face, using spacer ends, forming two crates which can take a good deal of hard knocks without in any way damaging the models. With a little care, the various buildings can interlock, reducing the space between the boards appreciably. One of the smaller linking board is dropped so that the track

Bridge on dropped baseboard

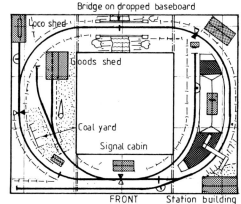

Loco shed

Goods shed

Plan No. SP4:

4ft 6in × 3ft 6in:

Minimum radius 1ft 3in

Coal yard

Signal cabin

FRONT   Station building

3

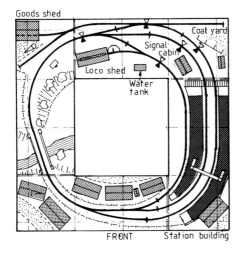

Plan No. SP5:

4ft 6in × 4ft 6in:

Minimum radius 1ft 3in

can bridge a valley, a simple way of getting a valued scenic effect.

As the platform is an island, access is by means of a footbridge, the main station building being on the corner of the baseboard. Two trains can be easily accommodated on this system, there is scope for reasonably authentic operation and, once again, the best running is anticlockwise.

SP5 uses four identical sized baseboards and can not only handle up to three trains, but will cope with either clockwise or anticlockwise operation. Inevitably, the potential is limited, but that is one of the crosses one has to accept when working in very small spaces. There is reasonable scope for scenic modelling.

Whilst I have not shown baseboard joints on SP6, there would be little dif-

ficulty in breaking the model down into sections, though I did envisage this as a permanently erected model, possibly in a garden shed with a door in the front.

Its most interesting feature is that, unlike all previous plans, this is designed for possible two-operator use. As there is no run-round loop in the terminus, it will be essential to have a spare locomotive, sitting in the loco shed, to take the coaches out, releasing the train engine. One has the choice of changing locomotives or of backing the coaches into the other platform and then, after the shunter is safely back in its shed, putting the train engine back. At the through station, the loco is uncoupled and sent completely round the main line to reverse the train. Whilst wholly unprotypical, it is the simplest way round a train on so small and simple a layout.

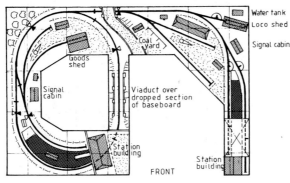

Plan No. SP6:

6ft 0in × 4ft 0in:

Minimum radius 1ft 3in

4

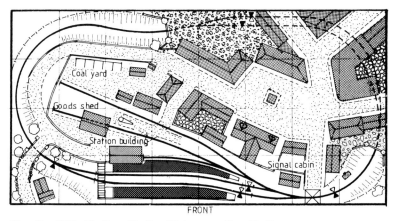

Plan No. SP7: 8ft 0in × 4ft 0in: Minimum radius 1ft 6in

2: Eight Feet Wide

Our American cousins are very fond of an 8ft × 4ft layout, largely because this happens to be the standard size of a sheet of man-made material, ply, chipboard or semi-hardboard. As many American homes have large basements, such a board can be stood on trestles in the centre of an otherwise under-utilised space.

In Britain cellars are rare and so we tended to favour 6ft × 4ft boards, which are in my opinion a poor compromise, too big to be easily housed, too small for most purposes. However, I feel we dismissed the 8ft by 4ft approach too casually, for the major-ity of garages are this wide and, with modern cars, it is generally possible to carry a baseboard over the bonnet height at the end of the garage.

There are several good reasons for this arrangement. One is not only utilising space which would otherwise be wasted, but also getting a bulky item out of the domestic quarters, reducing family friction. Any mess produced during construction will cause no quarrels and be readily cleared away whenever convenient.

As garages are utilitarian structures, whatever you do to create the scenery must

Plan No. SP8: 8ft 0in × 4ft 0in: Minimum radius 1ft 6in

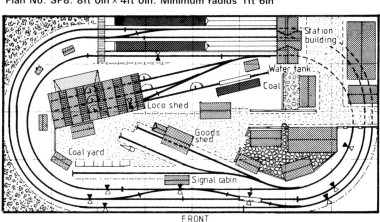

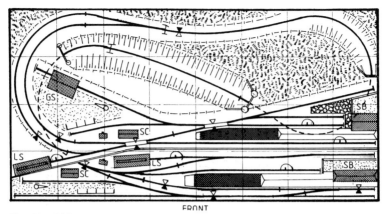

FRONT

Plan No. SP9: 8ft 0in × 4ft 0in: Minimum radius 1ft 3in

be an improvement, whilst the fact that the windows, if any, are generally small, enables one to create a night effect on a scenic model. All in all, the garage width layout has a good deal going for it.

SP7 shows a very simple scheme, too simple for most enthusiasts, I fancy. It comprises a basic single-track passing station with two goods sidings, with a set of hidden loops under a hill. This is a case of a model landscape with railway rather than a pure model railway, for we have room for a small village square close to the station.

It would appear that the hidden tracks are totally inaccessible and a potent source of trouble, but this is not so. This layout should not be built on a single sheet of material, but instead there should be a large hole in the main framing where the village square is situated. The architectural models are built on a lighter framing carried several inches above the main level, so that by ducking underneath the builder can get to the tracks or, if heavy maintenance is required, the entire village section can be lifted off in sections.

This not only improves the access but allows the modeller to work on the structures in the comfort of the living room, in the bosom of his, or her family.

SP8 is the complete antithesis of the previous plan, a double track main line with an inner multi-purpose line whence trains can easily be transferred. All shunting is carried out at the front of the board, and the main movement at the less accessible rear is confined to loco movements, where, given halfway decent tracklaying

Plan No. SP10: 8ft 0in × 4ft 0in: Minimum radius 1ft 3in

FRONT

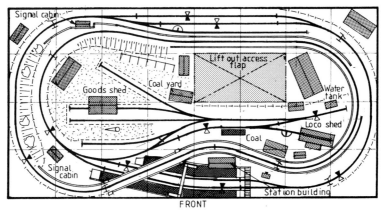

FRONT

Plan No. SP11: 8ft 0in × 4ft 0in: Minimum radius 1ft 3in

and well maintained stock, there should be no problems. The high-level road section should be removable for access to the tracks below.

In SP9 we have a terminus-to-terminus scheme arranged as a spiral. The two termini have been made as different as possible to add interest to operation. The rear landscape is fairly simple, largely because the high level terminus will cut off most of the view. I envisage tank engines or diesel locomotives as no turntables are feasible.

SP10 provides an out and back scheme with ample scope for scenic development beyond the single, rather elementary terminus. The most interesting feature is the high level continuous run which forms the reverse loop feed section. In practice, if this is fed from an independent controller,

the usual electrical complications of the reverse feed will not be apparent to the operator — in computerese, the change-over is transparent to the user.

In SP11 we have a looped eight scheme with spare loops on the rear road. These are normally inaccessible, but as they will be heavily used, it will be necessary to get to them from time to time, so a lift-out access flap is shown just large enough for someone of normal girth to stand inside in comfort. There is, of course, absolutely no need to have any cover at all at this point; indeed, if one gets away from the concept of a single sheet of board as the base of the layout, it is obvious that the access space could be slightly larger and provide room for the operator, allowing viewers to study the layout from the front.

Plan No. SP12: 8ft 0in × 4ft 0in: Minimum radius 1ft 3in

7

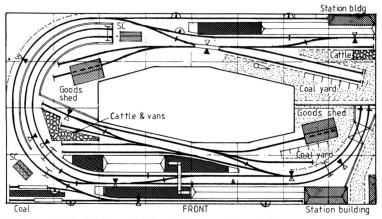

Plan No. SP13: 8ft 0in × 4ft 0in: Minimum radius 1ft 3in

The value of an operating/access space inside a layout is such that we should take the idea further. SP12 is another spiral point-to-point but arranged on two pairs of rectangular baseboards. This is not a portable scheme as such; with multiple levels each section is quite bulky and I envisage the model being erected at the back of the garage, being taken down only when called upon to appear at shows or in the event of a move, when it should be a matter of utter simplicity to re-erect the whole thing in the new garage and have trains running long before the house is straight — providing one has the nerve!

Both termini are provided with turntables, there is moderate scope for scenic development and, whilst the total capacity is relatively small, the owner could get a good deal of enjoyment from such a model.

SP13 has a low-level continuous double track main line with a single-track branch to a high-level terminus. Were I building this scheme, I should certainly try to provide storage loops beneath the high-level station which, naturally, would be on a separate sub-base that could be lifted off for maintenance, probably in two sections. The gradients are fairly complex, as the main line drops to provide extra clearance for the tracks.

The layout is suitable for two-operator working, the man inside operating the terminus, the outer operator concentrating on the main line.

SP14 is another out-and-back scheme with a large and impressive high-level terminus. The inner of the two rising tracks

Plan No. SP14: 8ft 0in × 4ft 0in: Minimum radius 1ft 3in

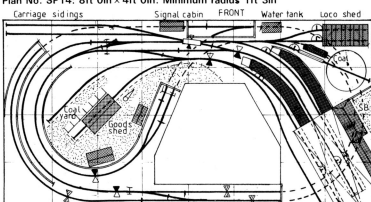

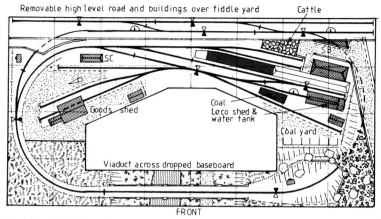

Removable high level road and buildings over fiddle yard   Cattle

SC

Goods shed

Coal
Loco shed &
water tank

Coal yard

Viaduct across dropped baseboard

SB

FRONT

Plan No. SP15: 8ft 0in × 4ft 0in: Minimum radius 1ft 3in

sets the critical gradient; clearance under the terminus throat will be tight and so, although this scheme offers a very high potential, with four-coach trains, large locomotives, a reasonable amount of storage for stock and the pleasure of a continuous run on which you can let your trains rip, it should only be tackled if you are up to the involved baseboard construction. A tip here is to build a small scale model of the layout beforehand to see exactly how the gradients are arranged.

SP16 is an example of a single-track branch with the fiddle yard devised by Maurice Deane, arranged behind a back-

scene which, in this case, is a retaining wall topped with a removable roadway. The location of the crossovers in the fiddle yard is critical if the maximum storage capacity is to be achieved.

If one can extend the depth of the end-garage site to five feet (or more) the scope of the model is considerably enhanced. Widening any of the previous layouts will clearly improve matters, but an even better arrangement is to have the last two feet or so as hidden loops and access space. This is shown to advantage in SP17 where, for the first time in over 40 years, I have managed to get all the elements of a

Plan No. SP16: 8ft 0in × 4ft 0in: Minimum radius 1ft 3in

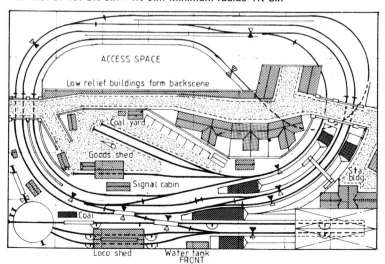

ACCESS SPACE

Low relief buildings form backscene

Coal yard

Goods shed

Signal cabin

Coal

Sta.
bldg.

Loco shed   Water tank
FRONT

9

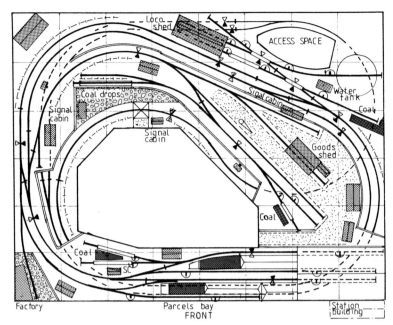

Plan No. SP17: 8ft 0in × 6ft 0in: Minimum radius 1ft 10in

favourite scheme for a through terminus in proportion simply by getting the operator outside the layout proper and having all the convoluted tracks needed to enable the line to be conveniently operated set behind the low relief backscene.

As this large and impressive station (by model standards) is clearly a major railway centre, it has a full urban setting, with rows of buildings forming the visual end of the modelled scene. A sky backscene on the walls beyond, possibly no more than a coat of emulsion paint on hardboard, provides the finishing touch. The visual curves are fairly easy but behind the bridges marking the limit of 'reality' we get down to the 15in minimum compatible with modern ready-to-run stock.

SP18 is almost all railway, and whilst in

no way a copy of any actual prototype, follows a common prototype arrangement where the goods yard and loco depot are some way along the line from the passenger terminus. The operator stands in the middle and is able to reach all essential tracks with ease, whilst all turnouts are exposed.

As almost all space is taken up, I've shown the station building as an intrusion into the viewing space in an end garage situation. If, as is sometimes the case, one has a slightly longer than usual garage, or the family car is a super-mini, the low level tracks could with advantage be brought out in front of the high level terminus. Once again, this is a scheme where a small scale model could be produced before construction begins.

3: The Garden Shed

The economics of the garden shed are such that, if one is buying one primarily for a layout, there is little point in getting a small one, for when the cost of providing proper foundations, laying a dry all-weather path and, above all, providing an electricity supply in accordance with regulations is taken into consideration, the

difference between a 6ft × 4ft store and a decent-sized structure is relatively small.

However if an existing shed is available, then it can be pressed into use. These two plans are for a nominal 7ft × 5ft shed, the smallest size in which a halfway decent layout can be built. Since sizes are taken externally, we have roughly 6ft 6in by

10

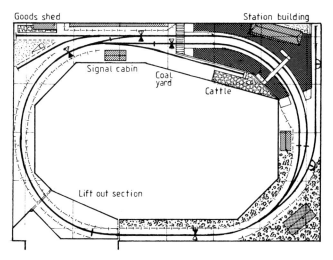

Goods shed   Station building

Signal cabin

Coal yard

Cattle

Lift out section

Plan No. SP18: 6ft 6in × 4ft 6in: Minimum radius 1ft 10in

4ft 6in inside.

SP18 is based on a layout I built some years back and is essentially a developed test track around a small workshop. Despite the small size, all turnouts, bar that in the goods yard, were large radius, mostly curved pattern. The end product was a very good looking, smooth running test track and an excellent test bed for kit-built locomotives.

SP19 is a more ambitious scheme with a four-track sector plate fiddle yard at the lowest level. The station represents the terminus of a single-track steam-age branch serving a small market town. I've provided a turntable since there are now so many excellent tender locos available which are right for this type of line. Note that the low-level tracks are kept clear of the table, for even the GWR pattern with its shallow well needs some form of mechanism underneath, whilst the more usual type of under girder table projects well below baseboard level.

Plan No. SP19: 6ft 6in × 4ft 6in: Minimum radius 1ft 10in

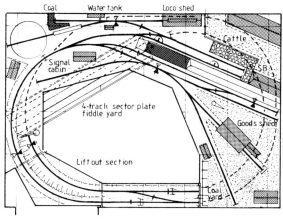

Coal   Water tank   Loco shed

Cattle

Signal cabin

SB

4-track sector plate fiddle yard

Goods shed

Lift out section

Coal yard

11

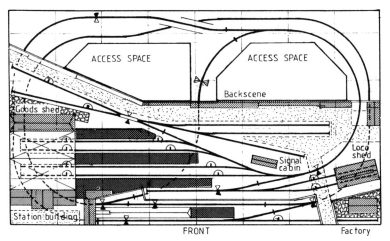

FRONT   Factory

Plan No. SP20: 8ft 0in × 4ft 6in: Minimum radius 1ft 3in

4: Continental Excursion

SP20 is an urban terminus, with the backscene that disguises the rear loops made from a selection of the lovely building kits one can find in the better model shops.

This layout would not be completely out of place in a modern British scheme, but SP21 is quintessentially Swiss, with a goods loop near to the station buildings and a pair of passing tracks beyond. The station is modelled as a junction, with the inevitable scissors crossing and double slip.

Plan No. SP21: 8ft 0in × 5ft 0in: Minimum radius 1ft 6in

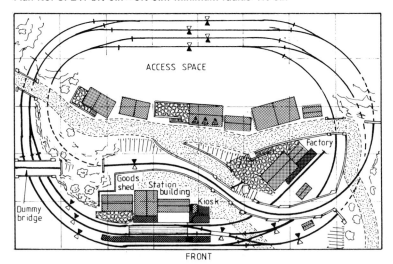

FRONT

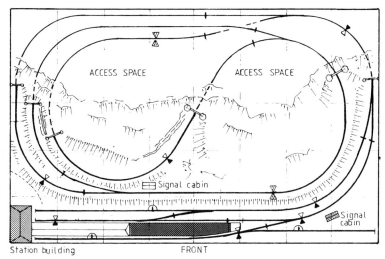

Station building   FRONT

Plan No. SP22: 8ft 0in × 5ft 0in: Minimum radius 1ft 6in

5: Into the Diesel Era

With the wide range of diesels now available for OO gauge, coupled with a good selection of BR coaching stock, it is hardly surprising that so many enthusiasts are turning to the diesel era for their prototype. Providing one is prepared to accept a three or four coach loco-hauled train, the simplification of track layouts, absence of

Plan No. SP23: 8ft 0in × 6ft 0in: Minimum radius 1ft 10in

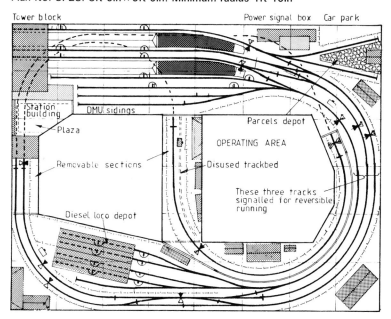

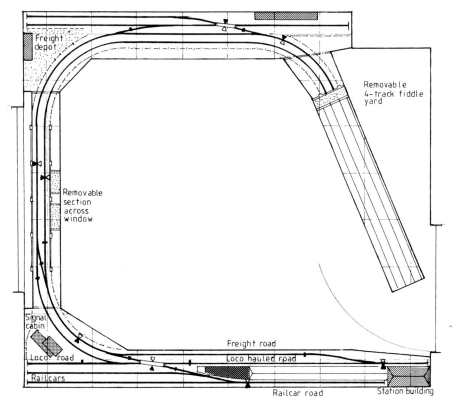

Plan No. SP24: 9ft 0in × 8ft 0in: Minimum radius 1ft 10in

turntables and coaling facilities and reduction in goods traffic fits well with the confines of a model layout and, as I shall show, the end-of-garage site is well suited for this type of model.

SP22 goes a stage further by following a prototype where three-coach loco-hauled trains were the norm until recently, the Highland division of ScotRail. The layout is the soundly based out-and-back with continuous run with a mountainous expanse of scenery. I've shown it on a 5ft-deep site, allowing fairly easy curves in the visible sections and a reasonable access space beyond. There is little scope for freight traffic, as it's all gone onto the inadequate roads!

SP23 again loses freight traffic, but does provide for parcels services and has not only a diesel MPD but standing sidings for DMU sets. Three features of modern track layout are incorporated: a series of ladder crossovers, reversible running on all three approach roads to the terminus and the 'narrowing' of a former double track section to single track, simulated by the provision of a double width road bed.

SP24 is designed to fit a room I had in my youth, and shows how a double track main line system can be fitted onto quite narrow shelving around a small room and leave ample space to allow it to be used as a bedroom. Freight operation is a trifle improbable: the trains run to the terminus to be run round, then proceed to the sidings which I suggest should not be too closely identified with any one of the current specialised block train freights so that, according to your whim, you can run any type of special purpose wagon.

The terminus and freight yard are fixed units, there is a removable fiddle yard and a viaduct section, also removable, spanning the window.

14

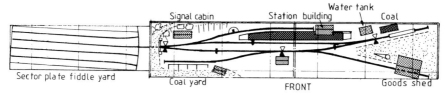

Plan No. SP25: 9ft 0in × 1ft 3in: Minimum radius 2ft 6in

6: The Fiddle Yard

The purpose of the fiddle yard is to provide a means of holding a number of complete trains and reversing them to enable an authentic timetable to be run over the 'real' portion of the layout. Most exhibition layouts today incorporate some form of fiddle yard and those interested in the system cannot do better than to visit their local show and study the system in action. Since the fiddle yard will be the key to all the succeeding plans, it is appropriate to look a little more closely at the many possibilities.

The most popular arrangement for small termini is undoubtedly the sector plate, where any one of a number of tracks laid on a suitable pivoted board can be aligned with the entry/exit road. SP25 shows such a yard coupled to a small branch terminus. This is in practice about the simplest layout one can build that will hold interest for any length of time. The track passes under an overbridge where it leaves the 'real' world; this is a more probable arrangement than the tunnel employed on the earliest schemes.

SP26 shows a completely self-contained system on three 3ft-long baseboards, with a small factory and the local coal yard in front of the sector plate. You will see a lot of layouts following this general plan at exhibitions, with the operators behind the backscene. In the home, they change sides, the control panel being independent of the baseboards.

Another arrangement of fiddle sidings is shown in SP27, where the storage roads are fed by a kickback track. The virtue of this arrangement is that any shunting in and out of the station takes place on this road and does not mean that one storage road has to be left clear.

In all these cases the locomotives are lifted off the track and placed at the other end of the train by hand. Where space permits, an unencumbered traverser can be converted into a train turntable. This presents few problems at exhibitions but can be awkward in the home where the layout has to be placed close to a wall.

In SP28 we have a continuous circuit with a traverser fiddle yard. It will be seen

Plan No. SP26: 9ft 0in × 2ft 0in: Minimum radius 2ft 6in

Plan No. SP27: 9ft 0in × 1ft 6in: Minimum radius 2ft 6in

15

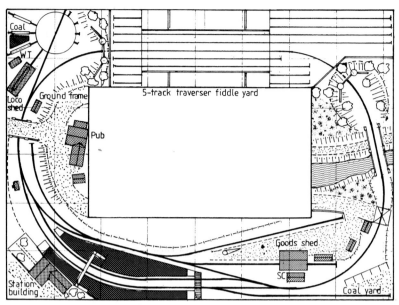

Plan No. SP28: 8ft 3in × 6ft 0in: Minimum radius 2ft 0in

that there is room for quite a bit of storage off the traverser, enabling this layout to accommodate an extremely large number of quite short branch line trains. There is standing for four complete trains off the fiddle yard itself in the top right corner.

The little loco depot in the top left has the standard 65ft dia turntable, but if anyone is modelling this layout I would suggest a 50ft or 55ft would be a better

proposition. The station plan is based on a fairly common arrangement on the later cross country lines, where a complete goods loop was situated on the far side of one of the platforms. This is if anything more useful on a model than it was on the prototype.

SP29 shows the Deane pattern fiddle yard, situated behind the terminus and hidden by a removable backscene. The

Plan No. SP29: 6ft 0in × 4ft 0in: Minimum radius 1ft 6in

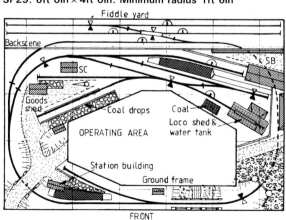

16

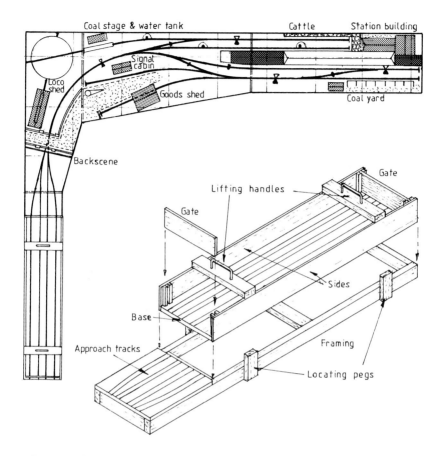

Plan No. SP30: 8ft 3in × 7ft 0in: Minimum radius 2ft 0in

whole purpose of this is to present a pleasing picture when the layout is not in use. During the actual running, the operator is well aware that he is storing trains directly behind the station and the backscene only gets in the way. There is reasonable scope for scenic modelling in what is by any standards a very small area and, with everything in easy reach of the operator, this type of layout is extremely convenient.

The final scheme shows the Denny pattern fiddle yard. Here a series of points fan out to feed a set of storage roads. There are two possibilities: the entire storage module lifts off and can be turned end for end or, where the configuration permits, the system forms a large train turntable.

The system demands a carefully planned timetable so that reversal of the storage unit only occurs at roughly one hour intervals. The point entry allows the entire operation to be remotely controlled from the main control panel.

A further possibility is the provision of two or more complete magazines so that a much larger collection of trains can be assembled and brought into use as required.

The terminus incorporates a turntable shed, which is accessed through the cattle dock road. It is not a good idea to take a loco shed road directly off a terminal bay, since it is impossible to gain access to the shed whilst a train is standing in the bay road. This is brought about by the fact that, in the model, the bay roads are much shorter than on the prototype.

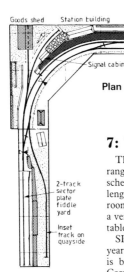

Goods shed   Station building   Water tank
Coal

Signal cabin

2-track
sector
plate
fiddle
yard

Inset
track on
quayside

Plan No. SP31: 6ft 9in × 4ft 9in: Minimum radius 2ft 0in

7: The Classic L

The L formation is a very popular arrangement for a terminus-fiddle yard scheme, as it not only enables a fairly lengthy layout to fit into a normal-sized room, but also adds stability to the model, a very important consideration where portable layouts are involved.

SP31 is based on a layout I built many years ago in an under-stairs cupboard, and is based on the old station at St. Ives, Cornwall. It was quick to build and proved quite interesting to operate. The fiddle yard section stretched across the corridor and was linked by the usual split hinges, which enabled me to swing it out of the way when needed.

SP32 takes the same basic plan and adds the viaduct and loco yard from St. Ives, but departs in detail from the prototype in many respects, not the least the industrial siding masking the fiddle yard. The sector plate can swing behind the hollow backs of the low relief buildings. I have shown a small loco shed for an industrial tank loco, more because it's fun than from any real need for such a unit in so simple a setup.

SP33 is a more ambitious design. The terminus is quite extensive and the loco depot is provided with a turntable so that tender locomotives can be employed in a realistic fashion. The fiddle yard is fed by a single three-way turnout, a slightly different approach than previously employed.

Most L schemes are for single track systems but, as SP34 shows there is no real reason for this since in a none-too-lavish area a very pleasing double track terminus can be arranged.

There are several points to note, of

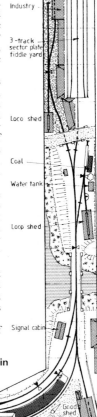

Industry

3-track
sector plate
fiddle yard

Loco shed

Coal

Water tank

Loco shed

Signal cabin

Station building

Good
shed

Coal yard

Plan No. SP32: 12ft 0in × 6ft 6in: Minimum radius 2ft 0in

18

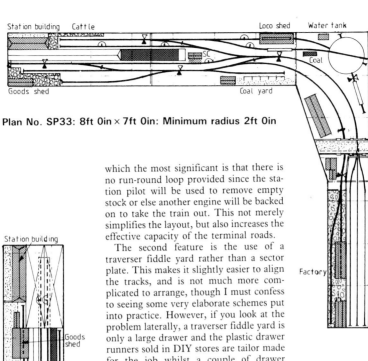

Plan No. SP33: 8ft 0in × 7ft 0in: Minimum radius 2ft 0in

which the most significant is that there is no run-round loop provided since the station pilot will be used to remove empty stock or else another engine will be backed on to take the train out. This not merely simplifies the layout, but also increases the effective capacity of the terminal roads.

The second feature is the use of a traverser fiddle yard rather than a sector plate. This makes it slightly easier to align the tracks, and is not much more complicated to arrange, though I must confess to seeing some very elaborate schemes put into practice. However, if you look at the problem laterally, a traverser fiddle yard is only a large drawer and the plastic drawer runners sold in DIY stores are tailor made for the job whilst a couple of drawer handles on each end provide a simple means of moving the unit bodily sideways.

The third point is that although there is a turntable, there is no loco shed. This arrangement was quite common in the steam age, where a table and a couple of standing roads would be provided at a terminus to enable locomotives with a short turn round time to be serviced quickly.

Plan No. SP34: 10ft 6in × 8ft 0in: Minimum radius 2ft 0in

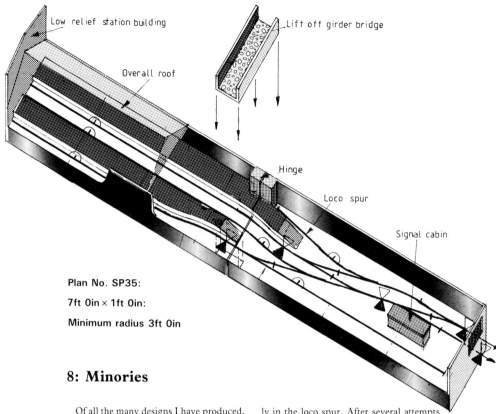

Low relief station building

Lift off girder bridge

Overall roof

Hinge

Loco spur

Signal cabin

Plan No. SP35:

7ft 0in × 1ft 0in:

Minimum radius 3ft 0in

8: Minories

Of all the many designs I have produced, none has caught the imagination of enthusiasts more than the deceptively simple Minories, a three-platform city terminus built on a pair of folding baseboards. I have lost count of the number of people who have approached me at exhibitions and informed me that they had built and enjoyed operating it.

The basic plan is shown in SP35, as in the original, as a quasi-isometric plan, showing the arrangement of retaining walls, overall roof and the lift-off overbridge spanning the end of the platforms. The new plan has an extra storage road added and the coal stage has been removed since the scheme is even more applicable to the diesel era than it was to the steam age in which it was conceived.

The original concept was inspired by the former arrangement at Liverpool Street (Met) which had two running roads and a long bay which, in the days of the Met electric loco-hauled trains, was used to turn Aylesbury trains, which meant that one of those lovely Bo-Bo's sat permanent-

ly in the loco spur. After several attempts to turn it into a compact terminus, all of which ended up hopelessly entangled, I doodled a design incorporating a pair of crossovers which clicked — and have since spent 30-odd years trying, in vain, to improve upon the basic scheme.

The original scheme envisaged passenger services worked by tank locomotives, goods being dealt with further along the line, a normal arrangement in urban areas. However, I felt that many enthusiasts would prefer a complete set of facilities and a further design was produced. SD36 is a distinctly better arrangement than the original where goods trains had to run into a platform road. Here, in much the same space, we have an independent goods road with a couple of sidings off. As this is a diesel era layout, these sidings are shown as the parcels depot. For steam age working I'd confine these roads to van traffic, as this is more in keeping with the location than general goods.

In SP37, Minories has been transferred to the end-of-garage site and provided with

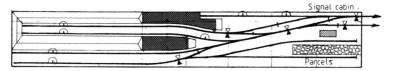

Plan No. SP36: 8ft 0in × 1ft 3in: Minimum radius 3ft 0in

an out-and-back stretch of line, with a large motive power depot fitting neatly into the reverse loop. A little modeller's license has been indulged in, as not only is the location between a pair of running roads completely unprototypical, but there ought to be an independent shunting spur to enable all shed movements to take place clear of the busy main lines. As this is a steam age layout, a conventional goods yard is provided, the former loco spur has become a parcels bay and an extra loco spur is stuck into the corner to hold a station pilot.

The differential between the platform lengths is also rather more marked than on the original: the two shorter roads would be used for local traffic, with tank locomotives hauling three non-corridor coaches, the longer road being used for the semi-fast trains comprising four corridor coaches headed by a 4-6-0.

The loco depot is provided with a four-track shed, with standing for two further

locos outside the shed, a 'cripple road' where two locos needing attention can stand and a long siding in the front where the breakdown train would normally stand. The cripple road is useful, on an intensively worked model, as a place to park those locomotives that are starting to play up, so that they can be dealt with in comfort during a maintenance session.

It could be argued that the locomotives provision is very much out of proportion, on a purely logical basis, and this is perfectly true. However, railway modelling only appears to be a logical hobby, and in practice we do things for irrational reasons and then scamper round looking for prototype justification. The simple fact is that most of us will gladly opt for a loco stud 100% in excess of our needs. So, acknowledging the fact that the layout will be overloaded with locomotives, I've provided somewhere to put some of them whilst producing a motive power depot of quite modest dimensions.

Plan No. SP37: 8ft 0in × 5ft 0in: Minimum radius 1ft 6in

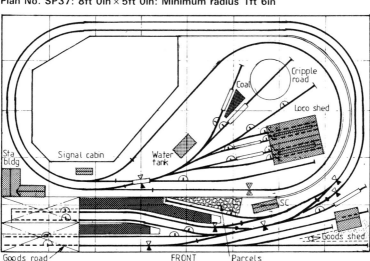

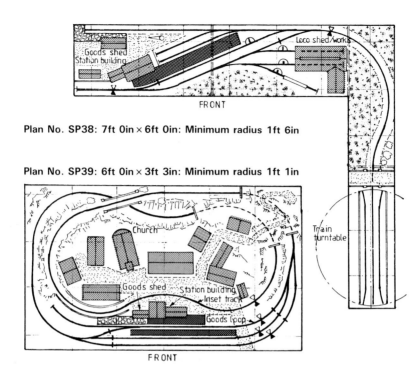

Plan No. SP38: 7ft 0in × 6ft 0in: Minimum radius 1ft 6in

Plan No. SP39: 6ft 0in × 3ft 3in: Minimum radius 1ft 1in

9: Narrow Gauge

Plan No. SP40: 8ft 0in × 4ft 0in: Minimum radius 9in

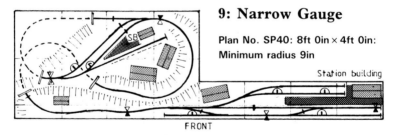

Narrow gauge railways make very good minimum space layouts, combining as they do sharper than standard curves and, in many cases, appreciably shorter trains.

SP38 keeps to fairly easy curves, but trains are restricted in length, hence the provision of a full train turntable as a fiddle yard is in order. As such lines are self-contained, the loco shed also incorporates a workshop. The scheme is for a four-baseboard portable line.

We turn to the Swiss metre gauge for SP39, a looped eight with one track inset in the road in front of the only station. I look on this more as a trial effort to find out if one wants to go fully into this field, for with up to 14-coach trains on the Rhaetian railway, one really can't talk of short trains and to get the full effect of these spectacular lines one really needs a good deal of room.

The third scheme SP40, is for a compact 009 line partly in a chimney recess with the terminus over the mantlepiece. Something of the spirit of the Welsh slate railways could be introduced into this model.

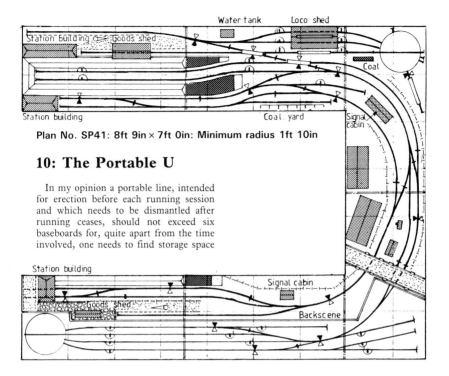

Plan No. SP41: 8ft 9in × 7ft 0in: Minimum radius 1ft 10in

10: The Portable U

In my opinion a portable line, intended for erection before each running session and which needs to be dismantled after running ceases, should not exceed six baseboards for, quite apart from the time involved, one needs to find storage space for the layout between running sessions.

The U-shaped terminus-fiddle yard is an excellent arrangement, for on three pairs of rectangular baseboards 3ft 6in long by 1ft 6in wide, there is room to model a large terminus with a branch heading off to shield the fiddle yard. This is yet another variant; the tracks converge on a turntable and a number of loco-holding tracks are provided for the stud.

The terminus is, a three-platform passenger station capable of handling up to four-coach trains coupled with a reasonably sized goods yard. The main line is double tracked, though it reverts to single the moment it passes under the overbridge and into the imaginary world of the fiddle yard. The fact that the coal yard is across the tracks from the rest of the freight facilities makes for some interesting moves.

The little single-track branch can be treated as a completely self-contained section, which under the pressure of exhibition working could be highly convenient. However, it is possible to run directly from the branch into any of the station tracks.

The loco depot has a double ended two-road shed and an avoiding line. Its location reduces the effective length of the further goods siding but as some 30in of siding space is still available, this is not really an onerous restriction.

The branch is modelled as a through station with one long siding, with a suggestion of double track disappearing under the road overbridge and high level station building. The track arrangement is, shall we say, different.

This layout is designed with possible exhibition in mind, and if anything the view from the outside is better than that gained by the operator inside. Two sets of removable backscenes would be needed to ring the changes from home to hall.

I have attempted to get away from the more usual country branch theme and show the sort of layout where an intensive service of trains of all types would not look out of place. Although the standard 65ft turntable does preclude Pacifics, there is room for a 75ft table and for once I feel that the larger locomotives would not look out of place.

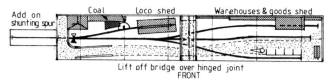

Plan No. SP42: 6ft 0in × 1ft 0in: Minimum radius 3ft 0in

11: Special Purpose

It is not obligatory to incorporate passenger facilities into a layout, and indeed there can be very real benefits when a small layout is designed around a specialised service.

The first of these schemes, SP42, is based on the 65-year-old portable scheme of A. R. Walkley, a simple goods yard on hinged baseboards with a short shunting neck added to increase the capacity of the model. Although a lot of fun can be had with this simple layout, I've shown the extension since this model can be linked into a larger system at a later date and the hole in the end backscene will prove very handy.

The same consideration applies to the loco depot, SP43, though I envisage this scheme as something for the enthusiast whose main interest lies in the construction of locomotives, whether scratchbuilt, from kits, adaptations of commercial models or a mixture of all three modes. The shed design is based on GWR practice for its smaller depots, hence the raised coaling stage with water tank over the building. However, the elements have had

to be compressed in order to get it all on the fairly generous allowance of three 3ft × 1ft 6in baseboards, which shows, I hope, how large steam age loco depots could be.

Finally in SP44 we have a rather more elaborate goods yard, again on three 3ft by 1ft 6in baseboards. I have not saturated the baseboards with tracks, as my aim was to leave enough room to allow the illusion that the wagons could be loaded and unloaded in the yards. I must confess that even so one would need to spot lorries or carts with care if it were not to be all too patently obvious that the space between the tracks is less than half what it should be.

It would make an excellent exhibition feature, either on its own, or as an adjunct to the club's larger layout. It is, I think, not fully appreciated by club members that it is fairly easy to arrange matters so that useful adjuncts, such as a goods yard or large loco depot, can be joined onto the main layout which, whilst restricted for room in the clubhouse, has space to spare when taken to the local hall.

Plan No. SP43: 9ft 0in × 1ft 6in: Minimum radius 2ft 6in

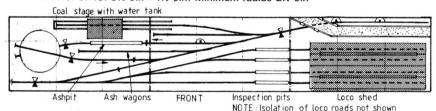

Plan No. SP44: 9ft 0in × 1ft 6in: Minimum radius 2ft 6in

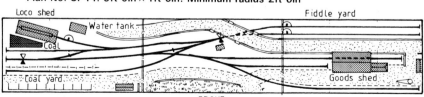

24

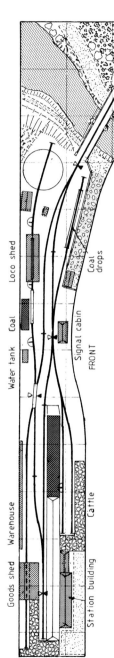

Plan No. SP45: 13ft 6in × 8ft 0in:

Minimum radius 2ft 0in

Loco shed

Coal drops

Water tank　Coal

Signal cabin

FRONT

Cattle

Goods shed　Warehouse

Station building

12: Country Termini

At one time enthusiasts were advised to model, as faithfully as possible, the last half mile of a country branch. Of late, this claim has become a little muted as a couple of awkward facts have filtered through. Of these, the subtle one is that this would only take the model up to the distant signal, if as far, since the warning signal is normally set half a mile in front of the outer home, which will itself be some distance from the end of the platform.

A more cogent difficulty is illustrated graphically in SP45 where, despite the fact that the model sprawls round two walls of a garage, the masking overbridge is little over a quarter of a scale mile from the buffers. If anyone likes to object that this is not really a small railway, I am not going to argue the point; my purpose was rather to emphasise the sheer size of a model branch line terminus if, as I think most people feel is desirable, we not only set out to handle four-coach trains, but want a length of unencumbered main line so that we can enjoy seeing our trains run through a section of rural landscape. Since, providing we have the fiddle yard on removable baseboards, the model will not impede the other purpose of the garage, housing the family car, I feel it is allowable within our rather flexible terms of reference.

The terminus is a conventional set-up, with one long platform, a shorter bay road, a couple of goods sidings and a simple loco shed with turntable, since with a four-coach train one can make good use of the many smaller tender locomotives now

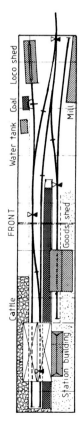

Coal　Loco shed

Water tank

Mill

FRONT

Goods shed

Cattle

Station building

Plan No. SP46: 8ft 0in × 1ft 3in:

Minimum radius 3ft 0in

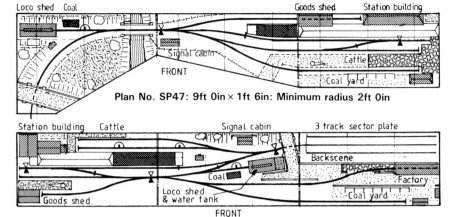

Plan No. SP47: 9ft 0in × 1ft 6in: Minimum radius 2ft 0in

Plan No. SP48: 9ft 0in × 1ft 6in: Minimum radius 2ft 6in

available. Clearly, like most interesting branch line models, this is a steam age project.

The line follows a ledge, rather than diving into a cutting, and this produces a pleasing effect with the train fully visible on a reasonably easy curve; the object of the scenic treatment here is to provide a setting for the trains. Reverting to that half mile, what we've done here is to compress the last half mile into roughly half the length whilst creating the illusion of a line of railway in open countryside.

Another idea put forward as the answer to all problems is to model an actual station. It has some severe disadvantages, which are exemplified in SP46, a somewhat compressed 4mm scale representation of Ashburton.

For a start Ashburton has no signal box, a serious omission. Then the mill siding is almost impossible to shunt with a locomotive; indeed, to the best of my knowledge, this was avoided on the prototype, wagons either being hauled by horses, or pulled along by a length of rope hitched to the locomotive on the parallel main line.

The advantage of the branch terminus is that it can be drastically reduced in size without serious loss of character and, with two-coach trains the norm, sensible operation to the prototype working timetable is feasible in a restricted space. This in my opinion is its greatest virtue. SP47, SP48 and SP49 are typical examples of the *genre* following tried and tested layout designs which provide for a selection of interesting train movements without creating too many snarl ups. SP49 also shows a possibility with a sectional layout, the inclusion of a small section of main line on an optional baseboard. This enables a line

Plan No. SP49: 8ft 6in × 1ft 3in: Minimum radius 2ft 6in

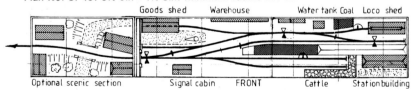

Plan No. SP50: 9ft 0in × 1ft 3in: Minimum radius 1ft 3in

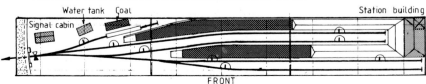

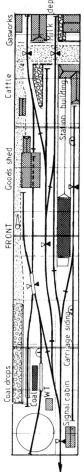

Plan No. SP51: 11ft 6in × 2ft 6in: Minimum radius 2ft 0in

which, in the home has to be fairly cramped, to spread itself when shown to the public in an exhibition hall.

Although single track branches are generally associated with steam, SP50 is suitable for early period diesel working. It is based on Fort William, where the original steam age station was later the terminus for loco-hauled diesel trains. I have added a long storage siding and a short loco spur to the bleak simplicity of the original since the model, unlike the prototype, does not have a large loco depot and sidings a little way down the line. The loco spur has rudimentary steam facilities shown; if a pure diesel scene were wanted then these could be modelled in a derelict condition.

Our final pair of single track termini are fairly large and are intended to allow for fully fledged branch line operation with 4-coach trains, strengthened, if desired with a van or two, as a norm. Provision is made for tender locomotives to be turned and there is scope for special purpose traffic.

SP51 has a large milk depot in the corner. Rather than have it running off the bay road, reducing the value of these lines, I have taken its lead directly from the run round loop and carried the line across two tracks with diamond crossings, a rare, but by no means unknown arrangement. Needless to say any suitable industry can be chosen, but with some excellent tankers on the market, milk is an obvious choice.

The goods yard is beyond the platform ends and the whole set up is jumbled about. One does sometimes get the impression that prototype branch termini were never planned, the various bits being left where they fell. I have tried to imply this in this model.

SP52 also has a rather muddled arrangement of freight facilities, but its nicest features are the two tracks crossing Station Road to the gasworks and dairy respectively. In each case the models are nominal rather than fully worked out; I'm assuming that, even in a garage location there are limits.

Plan No. SP52: 10ft 0in × 1ft 6in: Minimum radius 2ft 6in

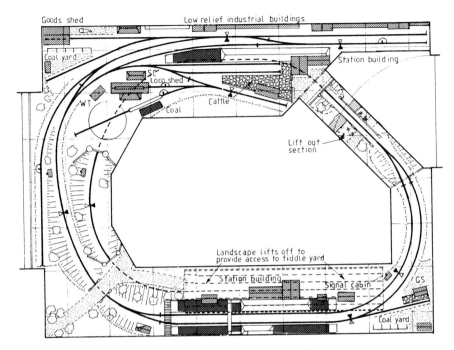

Goods shed Low relief industrial buildings

Coal yard

Station building

SC
Loco shed

WT Coal Cattle

Lift out
section

Landscape lifts off to
provide access to fiddle yard

Station building Signal cabin GS

Coal yard

Plan No. SP53: 9ft 0in × 7ft 0in: Minimum radius 2ft 0in

13: Branch Line

It is all very well to model a branch terminus but if the branch line bug bites hard the desire to reproduce rather more of this vanished feature of our railway system will arise. If it is to be at all satisfying then one needs a modest sized room and, I suggest, the layout should be a permanent feature and not made suitable for public exhibition.

SP53 is intended for a spare bedroom and is designed to handle four-coach trains headed by tender locomotives. I assume that the branch serves a reasonable sized country town with a certain amount of industry that grew up around the station which, as was very much the normal practice, was built on the outskirts of the town.

The goods yard is a trifle abbreviated but as there is one long siding which runs parallel to the industries, this is far less of a disadvantage than it appears at first sight. A more serious objection could be that the yard is at the extreme end of one's comfortable reach but this can be looked at

as a good way of teaching operators the virtue of careful shunting!

' The bay road is backed by a cattle dock, a pleasing set-up. I've not shown any isolation in the bay; either this is used by push-pull units or a diesel railcar, or it is treated as a parcels road. The loco depot is of medium capacity and has the standard 65ft diameter turntable. A storage siding, for spare coaches, is provided in the window recess.

The passing station is merely one long loop with rudimentary goods facilities but there is room to model the typical buildings of a country station. The line then crosses a small bridge on the lift-out section and dives under the approach road of the terminus, to emerge a little further round the layout before reaching the hidden fiddle yard. I have shown a sector plate here, and suggested that the landscape cover should be removable for operating convenience.

28

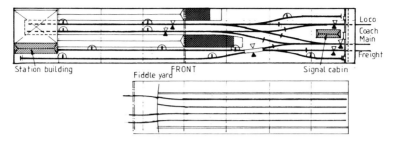

Plan No. SP54: 13ft 0in × 1ft 3in: Minimum radius 2ft 0in

14: City Stations

Although simple single track stations can be compressed, if you want a really compact layout you must look to the city, where space is as much at a premium as it is on our models. In this section I offer a number of city termini which not only justify intensive train operation but which do not call for artistic skills to create the scenery, since an urban setting implies brick or stone walls in all their myriad forms.

SP54 is based on a Freezer family layout, and although originally intended for the steam age, proved far better with diesel haulage. Although it appears to be double track, in actual fact it has a single line approach, and the other track is assumed to run into the freight yard. Both

end in the sector plate fiddle yard. Similarly, the loco/carriage siding also feeds into the fiddle yard. The idea is to simulate the operation one would see when watching the station throat. All yard movements are out of sight beyond the road bridge.

SP56 is another diesel era main terminus, purely loco hauled and DMU passenger trains with, perhaps, the occasional parcels train. The main feature is a varied platform length giving more space for a station building on those three 3ft by 1ft 6in baseboards I've used in previous schemes.

SP57 turns back the clock to steam days and calls for wider baseboards to allow for the turntable. One long platform is provided for the express trains, and it should be

Plan No. SP55: 9ft 0in × 1ft 6in: Minimum radius 2ft 6in

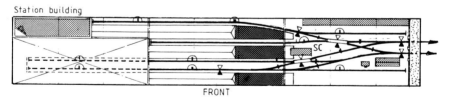

Plan No. SP56: 9ft 0in × 1ft 9in: Minimum radius 2ft 6in

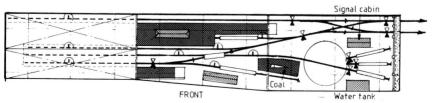

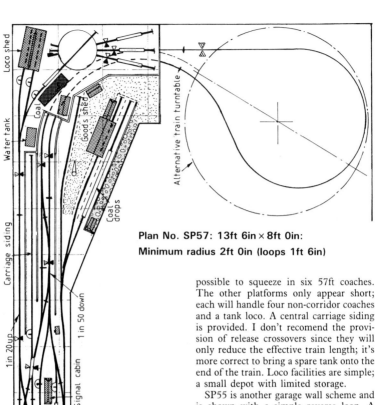

Loco shed

Water tank

Coal

Goods shed

Alternative train turntable

Coal drops

Carriage siding

1 in 50 down

1 in 20 up

Signal cabin

FRONT

Station building

Plan No. SP57: 13ft 6in × 8ft 0in:
Minimum radius 2ft 0in (loops 1ft 6in)

possible to squeeze in six 57ft coaches. The other platforms only appear short; each will handle four non-corridor coaches and a tank loco. A central carriage siding is provided. I don't recomend the provision of release crossovers since they will only reduce the effective train length; it's more correct to bring a spare tank onto the end of the train. Loco facilities are simple; a small depot with limited storage.

SP55 is another garage wall scheme and is shown with a simple reverse loop. A train turntable is shown chain dotted but this will restrict the total train length to four coaches. The facilities are reasonable; a single carriage siding, a modest goods yard with coal drops and a high level loco depot. Baseboard construction will be a trifle tricky, since the main line drops down between the goods yard and carriage siding whilst the loco road climbs. There are a lot of retaining walls!

SP58 is another design intended for a garage wall, but in this case I've omitted the turntable, assuming that the depot is along the line and that tender locos can be turned in the fiddle sidings. If diesel traction is preferred, the goods yard should be simplified, though I don't recommend that you follow the prototype slavishly and model the corner as a car park. When a large terminus is built on sectional bases, it is not difficult to ensure that at one joint both platforms and tracks cross at exactly a right angle. This allows one to include an optional extension to lengthen the trains, probably for exhibition purposes. SP59

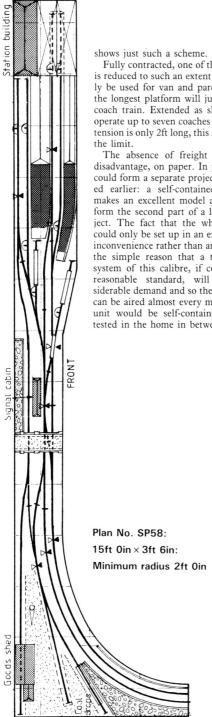

shows just such a scheme.

Fully contracted, one of the central bays is reduced to such an extent that it can only be used for van and parcel traffic, but the longest platform will just hold a five-coach train. Extended as shown one can operate up to seven coaches but, as the extension is only 2ft long, this is by no means the limit.

The absence of freight facilities is a disadvantage, on paper. In practice, these could form a separate project, as mentioned earlier: a self-contained goods yard makes an excellent model and this could form the second part of a long term project. The fact that the whole collection could only be set up in an exhibition is an inconvenience rather than an objection for the simple reason that a thoroughgoing system of this calibre, if completed to a reasonable standard, will be in considerable demand and so the whole system can be aired almost every month. As each unit would be self-contained, it can be tested in the home in between whiles.

Plan No. SP58:

15ft 0in × 3ft 6in:

Minimum radius 2ft 0in

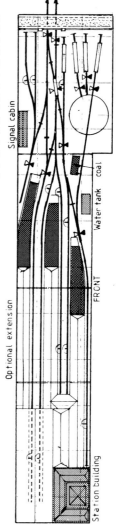

Plan No. SP59:

11ft 0in × 2ft 0in:

Minimum radius 2ft 6in

15: On Exhibition

Any sectional layout built to a reasonable level of competence can, with very little bother, join the exhibition circuit. Whether this is an advantage is open to question, for those of us who take part in this aspect of the hobby are gluttons for punishment, but there are few more satisfying ways of spending a week-end than with a small group of fellow enthusiasts putting something back into the hobby by demonstrating how a model railway should be run to several hundred happy members of the public.

A good exhibition layout should, in my opinion, not only be suited for public viewing, but be capable of being worked within the home so that thoroughgoing rehearsals can be carried out *before* the layout goes on public view. Any small faults should be traced and corrected in the build up to the show, every locomotive and piece of rolling stock should be tested and, where necessary, overhauled and, above all, the timetable must be run through several times not merely to train the operators, but to check that it works as it should.

At the same time, the viewing public must see the best side of the model, and the operators will stand or sit on the far side working the trains. This means that the controls are best arranged as a separate unit connected to the layout by means of multi-core cables and plugs.

Unfortunately, where the layout forms an L, the most convenient arrangement for the home, it is none too easy to fit it into an exhibition hall and give the public a proper view. This is where a frequently overlooked virtue of the sectional baseboard comes into play and so, in our final scheme, I show how it is possible to make a layout fit two different sites.

All we need is two different curves, one for the home, the other for exhibitions. Furthermore, to provide a bit of variety, they can be totally different in appearance, as I have shown in the designs. I've suggested that for an exhibition we replace an industry with a purely scenic feature, since the former tends to slow down operation and whilst, in the home, this is of no consequence, it is advisable at a public show to keep up a steady flow of trains at all times.

Furthermore, since there is more room available at a show, I've suggested that an additional baseboard with a harbour extension complete with flashing lighthouse is added. A word of warning: if you make additional sections for an exhibition, do let the organisers know the size of layout they are going to get. Nothing is more calculated to send an exhibition manager crazy than to discover that an exhibit he was assured was 16ft long now needs 18ft because the builder has added a bit to improve the model. This may well be true but if there is only 16ft feet available on the plan, something has to give. It is a well known fact that those who offend in this fashion also turn up half an hour before the show opens with the bland assurance that "it only takes 15 minutes to be up and running!"

Then they wonder why they're never asked again.

If, as I hope, you decide to build an exhibition standard layout, then do provide the organisers with accurate information and turn up in good time to erect the layout and test everything before the public arrive. Apart from anything else, if you do, you'll then have best part of an hour to preview the show and with any luck may pick up a bargain from the club's second hand stall or one of the traders.

Plan No. SP60: 15ft 0in × 2ft 9in: Minimum radius 2ft 0in